Taino
Zen

by Bobby González

Cemi Press - New York - www.cemipress.com
Bobby González - www.bobbygonzalez.com

Taino Zen
by Bobby González

Other books by Bobby González:
The Last Puerto Rican Indian: A Collection of Dangerous Poetry.
Puerto Rican Indian Wars: Part II
Song of the American Holocaust: Native Poetry from the South Bronx
Reservation

Cover Design and linocuts: Luis Cordero Santoni

ISBN 0-9785106-1-5
Library of Congress Control Number: 2006927293

Cemi Press
www.cemipress.com

Bobby González
www.bobbygonzalez.com
www.facebook.com/bronxtaino

To my one and only - Maria.

Contents

TAINO

Taino Zen

Taino Zen.
Still works the magic.
Has never stopped believing in the power.

Still works the magic
begun eons ago.
Two hundred fifty-two generations
in the past.

Taino Zen.
Reawakening.
Ancestral resurrection.

Taino Zen.
Cultural imperative.
Transformational journey.

Reconnect to the memories
without reactivating the anger.
Honor the trust and deliver the true message.

Who we were/who we are/who we will be.
Tribal poetry from warrior spirit
in the heart of the South Bronx Reservation.

Taino Zen.

Grandmother's House

A warrior's heart.
Tribal poetry from Indigenous Spanish Harlem.

In a room
on the second floor
of a tenement building
overlooking
the Cross Bronx Expressway
there lives an old woman
and her two cats.

Or is it
two cats and their old woman?

Doña Ramona
and
Caridad
and
Butch.

Her nemesis
is not old age.

Nor
Is the lack of human compassion
perceived
to be an adversary.

Doña Ramona
chants the dawntime prayer
her abuela had taught her
in the forbidden tongue.

She is care free
and
will light a corncob pipe
as soon as she finishes
brushing her lustrous silver hair.

Ode To Ibrahim Gonzalez

Mambo Dervish.

Awakened Spirit
continues his sacred journey on a higher plane.

Truth of a people.
Truth of a memory.
Our brother understood the language of the drum and shared its beauty.

He searched for an ultimate cosmic vision
in the blooming Bronx urban garden.

Ibrahim cleared a path for the rest of us to follow.
He invites us now to celebrate and enjoy life,
even with all of its challenges and tribulations.

Mambo Dervish.
Healer/dreamer/musical and poetic shaman.

He needed to speak out against injustice.
He needed to scream angrily.
He needed to laugh joyfully.
He needed to sing loudly.
He needed to cry
          And now so do we.

Gracias, Brother Ibrahim.
Walk in beauty, mi hermano.

River Song

Sing me a river song.
Take me to a distant shore.
Sing me a river song.
I need to travel far, far away.

Please, help me remember who I am.
Please, help me remember what I am.

Give rest to your feathered flute of old.
Transport me on the wings
of your vocal incantation.

On a raft fashioned out of hopes and memories,
carry my weary breast
across the unmasterable waters.

Singer/wayfarer/sorceror.

Work your charm.
Spin your magic.

Please, my uncle,
my mother's favored brother,
cast a melodious net
into the waters that have engulfed me
in a whirlpool of confusion and doubt.

Sing me a river song.
Calm my soul.
Sing me a river song.
Bless me with the strength not to let go
as I climb on the back of your melody
and fly straight as an arrow
on the back of your mysterious river song.

River Song – The Sequel

Winds of change.
Vientos de cambio.

Sister, sing me a river song.
Take me to a distant shore.
Hermana, sing me a river song.
I need to travel far, far away.

Navigate our people through uncharted waters.
Provide a guiding light through the thick and heavy darkness.
Careful – not to lose the old ways.
Careful – not to lose our people's natural rhythms.

Mother, sing me a river song.
Take me to a distant shore
Father, sing me a river song.
I need to travel far, far away

*****

El Río Camuy.
El Río Guajataca.

A long stretch of silence.

Broken by the sound of waves crashing on the shore

El Río Grande de Manatí.
El Río Grande de Arecibo.

Fragrance of tropical flora, moist fertility.
Light fragrance of river winds.
Smell the waters of Creation's village garden.

Ay, mi hermana, work your charm.
Spin your magic.
Por favor.
Cast a melodious net
into the waters that engulf us
in a whirlpool of doubt and confusion.

11

El Río Cibuco.
El Río Bayamón.
El Río Grande de Loíza.
El Río Espíritu Santo.

El Río Daguao.
El Río Humacao.
El Río Seco.
El Río Coamo.

Música de las aguas.
Canciones de los ríos.

Sing me a river song.

Calm my soul.

Bless me with the strength not to let go.

Canción del río.
Canción de amor.

Sing me a river song.
Sing me a song of love.

Orehu

His name was Maraka-Kore,
which translates as Red Rattle.
He was a semi-cici, a spiritual leader
of the Arawak.

Four young attentive children sat at his feet.
Maraka-Kore told the young ones
the story of the ancient Arawak chief
who was called Orowama.

"One day in the deep, deep past,
Orowama stood on the ocean shore
pondering upon the miseries
being experienced by his people."

"Just then, a beautiful woman emerged from the sea.
She was a physical manifestation
of Orehu,
Mother of the Waters.
Orehu. La Madre de las Aguas."

"She handed Orehu a branch
and told him to bury it.
That is how we received the calabash tree."

"She gave him the gift of tobacco
which had been unknown to us until then.
She gave him the gift of a feathered rattle,
the maraka.
She taught him many secrets and magical charms.
And then she withdrew into the sea."

This is an account of our Arawak relatives.
It is an old, old teaching story.
And we keep the myth alive
Because it belongs to us.

Every indigenous circle has its own unique spirituality.
We have ours.
And that is what makes us a distinct entity – TAINO.

Taino # 1

A thin wisp of tobacco smoke swirled up and across,
whipped about by an ocean breeze.

Frankie Mendoza popped a cigar out of his mouth
and
exhaled an oval shaped gray bush.

Frankie wasn't one for ceremonies,
especially those communal rituals.
He had never been in a sweat lodge
and
not once had he undergone a vision quest.
It wasn't his way of maintaining spiritual balance.

And yet here he was.
On the back porch of his brother's seaside shack.
Four days of fasting.
Four days of smoking.
Four days of waiting.
And nothing had happened.

There had been no new state of awareness.
No stupendous explosive insight.
Only a long boring stretch of silence,
broken only by the sound
of the waves of ocean water
washing up on the beach
and
by the sound of screeching seagulls
looking for a munchy handout.

Frankie stretched his arms out
and
took a healthy whiff of salty Caribbean air.
He felt the grains of sand
that had found their way
under his unwashed finger nails.

Frankie reached his point of exhaustion.
He fell on his aide
and fell asleep.
And that's when the adventure began.

His consciousness drifted to another plane
where he awakened to the whistling of a bone flute
and
the fragrance of pineapples and cedar trees.

The hosts of this party
made their presence known
with a shuffling of sandaled feet.

There they were – Frankie Mendoza's Taino ancestors,
just as they looked all those years ago.

Their skin tone
ranged from dark brown
to a gleaming yellow.
Each man in possession of the slender muscular build of
a master swimmer.
The beauty of the women emanated
from their intellect and their dignity.
A few children peeked from behind their parents' knees.
They smiled timidly.

Frankie Mendoza wept
at the feet of his ancestors.
Between sobs he apologizes
Because he did not resemble them physically
on account of centuries of miscegenation.
He wept because he was not able to speak
the ancient words which had been erased from his memory.
He wept because
he knew not the protocol appropriate
to welcoming the founders of his race.

A conch shell sounded in the distance
and
Frankie Mendoza raised his head.
Now it was his Taino forebears who wept.

In the language of the heart
they spoke to him.

"There is no reason to shed tears, our son,"
they said.
"There is no reason to mourn."
"Though you do not resemble us outwardly,
yet our people still live in you.
Ceremonies and protocol are important,
but they are not as significant
as simple sincerity
and
fearless pride in you who are."

"We believed that our people would one day be no more.
But you and your relations
are indisputable evidence
that our blood has endured."

"We thank you
for calling us with your prayers
and
honoring us
with your unwavering allegiance.

Frankie Mendoza sat up straight
and
opened his eyes.

He was now back in this world,
a world in which
he would no longer speculate
from day to day
on which wind
he would be leaving on.

As long as he kept
humility on either side of himself,
it would no longer matter where he was.
He knew who he was
and
from whence he came.

And that was what mattered.
and
that was all
that he needed.

That was all.

Price of the Gift

Sacramental act
taken in stride.
Exasperated Doña Suncha.

All flock to her
for guidance or healing.
Doña Suncha no longer belongs to herself.

Open-face woman
with androgynous cravings.
Vibrant woman steaming.
Object of curiosity.

Doña Suncha.
She needs love,
but she doesn't need ties.

El Yunque

El Yunque.
El Yunque.

Late in the evening,
the night owl,
the sinister múcaro,
ruffles its wings.

The spirits of the Dead
also awaken.
And they whisper in the wind:

Ma-bo-da-má-ka.
Ma-bo-da-má-ka.

Cotubanamá hu-pí-ya.
Cotubanamá o-pí-ya.

****

Sueña un trueno fuerte.

The sound of thunder

rumbles in the distance.

Secret language of the gods of night and mystery.

Yu-ca-jú Bagua Ma-o-ro-co-ti.
Yu-ca-jú Bagua Ma-o-ro-co-ti.

O-pi-yel-guo-bi-rán.

Deminan Cara-cara-col

El Yunque.
El Yunque.

Nature sprits manifest.
Time is a road taken in five directions.
Let the road take you.
Listen.
Listen!

*****

Na-bo-rí-a Da-ka.
Na-bo-rí-a Da-ka.

A-güey-ba-ná Ze-mi.
A-güey-ba-ná Ze-mi.

****

Yes.   Yes.

El Yunque.   El Yunque.

Listen,   Listen.

My ancestors call out.

My ancestors call out their own names.

Pú-po.
Yu-kí.
U-ra-yo-án.
Ya-hu-má-ra.
Ta-bó-a.
Gua-ro-kóo-yo.
Ya-ya.

****

From the land of shadows.
De un mundo oscuro.

Feel the pulsating earth
of El Yunque.
El Yunque.
Mi Madre Tierra.
La Tierra de Mi Madre.

El Yunque.
El Yunque.

Drums under the hills.
Drums under the hills.
They herald the approach of sunrise.

Melody prayer
of morning birds
bids farewell
to the departing
keepers of the mountains.

Los dueños de las montañas.

Ma-bo-da-má-ka.
Ma-bo-da-má-ka.

Cotubanamá hu-pí-ya.
Cotubanamá o-pí-ya.

EL YUNQUE.

El YUNQUE.

*Note: El Yunque is a mountain sacred to the Taino People. It is located on
the island of Borinkén (Puerto Rico).*

21

Wishful Thinking

If I
had been in circulation
back in 1492,
I would have stood up
to Christopher Columbus
and told him
to set up shop
in some other neck of the woods.

A-ta-bei-ra Gua-ka-ra-pi-ta

Con el permiso.
Con el permiso de Mis Antepasados.
With the permission of my ancestors.

Atabeira Gua-ka-ra-pi-ta es Mi Madre Diosa.
Atabei Mamona is my Mother Goddess.

Nuestros hermanos Africanos resan a Yemaya, Madre de todos los Orishas.
Our African sisters and brothes pay homage to Yemaya.

But we the Tainos of Borikén, Quisqueya y Cuba

23

call Atabeira <u>our</u> Mother of the Waters.
Nuestra Madre de Las Aguas.

Madre Diosa.
Mother Goddess.
Mother Creator.
Mother Protector.
Mother of us <u>all</u>.

She purifies the ocean with her tears.
She sanctifies the Earth with her holy menstrual blood.

First teacher.
Her original name is unspeakable.
AND ALL MOTHERS ENDURE PAIN UNKNOWABLE TO MEN.

Atabeira Gua-ka-ra-pi-ta.
El ritmo de la naturelaza.
The rhythm of Nature.
Red dirt of Borikén.
Atabei Mamona.

IT HAS BEEN SAID THAT THE CREATOR IS MUCH TOO INTELLIGENT
TO BE MASCULINE.

Red Woman.
Brown Woman.
Lives at the Source.

Atabeira Gua-ka-ra-pi-ta.
Atabei Mamona.

Mother, it is <u>so</u> sad.
The trees of the forest know where <u>their </u>roots lie,
but our children do not.

Ellos no saben de donde vinieron.
Ni saben pa' donde van.

Atabeira Gua-ka-ra-pi-ta.
Atabei Mamona.

Mistress of the Universe
sings soft words of remembrance.

Ofrendas left on the altar.
Ofrendas de tabaco, maíz y tabonuco.

Truth and memory.
La verdad y la memoria.

MAN ALWAYS FORGETS
THAT HE LACKS THE STRENGTH AND PATIENCE OF A WOMAN.

By reason of our color.
By reason of the land on which our grandmothers were born.
By reason of instructions given to us in dreams and visions.
By reason of whispers that come to us from the future.

Hear the words of the wind.
Listen to the dancing drum.

Atabeira Gua-ka-ra-pi-ta.

Atabeira Gua-ka-ra-pi-ta.
El ritmo de la naturelaza.
The rhythm of Nature.
Red dirt of Borikén.
Atabei Mamona.

The eternal Mother of us all.

Something to Think About

The original inhabitants of Puerto Rico,
Cuba, the Dominican Republic, et al.
had a carefully defined social order.

All adhered to an
unwritten set of laws.

And the system worked.

For though there were at least
several hundred thousand people on these islands,
there was not one jail, not one prison cell.

And though there were tens of millions of people
living on the land which is today called America,
there was not one penal institution in all this vast region.

Now that is what you call civilization.

Born facing the east.
Die facing the west
We must prepare ourselves.
The time has come.

Oración de Gracias
Thanksgiving Prayer

When was the last time you thanked God you were born a Puerto Rican?
¡Despierta, Boricua!
Wake up and smell the rice and beans.

Ponce. Rincón. Fajardo. Camuy.
Dale las gracias a Dios que nacíste puertoriqueño.

Some members of our family have shamefully tried
to deny our heritage, turning their backs on our precious blood heritage.

Bueno.
Está bien.

Como deciá mi abuela, "Allá ellos que son blancos."

Loíza. Utuado. Manatí. Yabucoa.

As for me …. I was born on the South Bronx Reservation.

Pero mis padres me enseñaron que Borikén es una nación sin fronteras.

And, every single morning when I wake up and see the beautiful sunlight,
I say quietly to myself:

"Thank God I was born a Puerto Rican."

Civilization

October 12, 1492.
The day that "civilization" came to town.
Not exactly a fortuitous "encounter."
One day the Earth will tell her side of the story.
Two thousand generations have their story, too.
Just you wait and listen.

October 12, 1492.
Uninvited guests with hidden agenda.
Believed us to be docile.
Believed us to be ignorant.
Believed us not to be in possession of real language.
Believed us not to have genuine valid spirituality.

October 12, 1492.
Annexed lands.
Annexed dreams.
Island people who once could never stop laughing.
Island people who once could never stop sharing.
Island people who once could never stop just living in the moment.
Island people who survived by moving in silence
                        by remaining invisible
                        hoping to be overlooked and forgotten.

World of shadows.
Standing by the wayside.
We who know which is the woman's direction and which is the man's.

Time to go back home.
Time to reclaim what is ours.

October 12, 1492.
The day "civilization" came to town.
Not exactly a "fortuitous" encounter.

In retrospect, it all happened just yesterday.
The day "civilization" came to town.

My People

Yolanda Lopez
calls her motorbike
her second husband.

She's a city warrior
and can always be found in the thick of the action.

Yolanda doesn't miss a trick.
When she curses you,
she can make the hairs
fall out of your ears.

Sometimes she falls asleep
with the memory
of the stench of burnt flesh.

Genetic memory.

Another side of life most people don't wanna know.

Bimini

Ponce de León
and company
eased on up
towards Florida
to look for
the Fountain of Youth.

Before they reached
the mainland,
however,
they stopped off
at a small island
to stock up
on fresh water
and whatever
available food
they could find.

Imagine their surprise
when they came upon
an old Indian woman
living on this isle alone.

It is still not clear
how she got there.
We still don't know
how she survived
for an extended period of time
without outside help.

She was one tough Taino Indian woman.

Still, she must have been lonely.

Voice of a Hero

In his idiosyncratic measure way of speaking,
Guamá addressed the hastily assembled army.

"It is time to revisit our dedication," he declared.
"It is time to renew our commitment."

He spoke to them about how the Spaniards had penetrated
the Cuban Sierras.
A batch of their soldiers could appear over the next hill any day now.
Time to wake up.
Time to rise up.

Guamá spoke on how even the very exhaled breaths of the newcomers
could kill them.
And no old medicine remedies concocted by their profoundly wise
grandmothers
would be able to save them.

Their extensive trade network had been disrupted.
Escape routes to the Ca-loo-sa up north
and to the Me-xi-ca of the west had been cut off.

The moon and the sun hovered side by side in the morning firmament.
Yet none in the ragtag regiment paid heed to the ominous celestial sign.

Guamá would eventually be betrayed by his own brother.
Like Tecumseh, Sitting Bull and Crazy Horse,
he would be sold down the river by a relative of the same blood, a child of
the same gods.

Guamá lifted a gourd drinking cup up to his lips
as the traitor stole out of the camp.

The traitor made plans as he plowed through the jungle underbrush.
The traitor made plans as he was being disowned by his Creator Mother.
The traitor made plans as his unfeathered hair flew in the wind.

And in short time, that same wind would be blowing away his bones.
And his cowardly voice would be forever silenced.
While a hero's voice still reverberates across the Cuban Sierras.
A voice, sturdy, unconquerable and true.   Guamá.   **31**

It's the Luck of the Draw

North of the White River,
a keeper of the flame
strikes a pose.

The majesty of his power
does not require validation
from the gringos/long knives/pale faces.

Meanwhile,
back at the ranch,
the Pilgrims have landed on Plymouth Rock.

Miles Standish
shouts out and exclaims,
"Boys, this continent is up for grabs!"

The Big Parade

It was a splendid pageant,
a parade of marvelous sights
that was conducted in the court of
King Ferdinand and Queen Isabela.
Christopher Columbus displayed the exotic bounty
which had been pilfered
from the so-called New World.

Among the flaunted specimens
were beautifully painted Natives,
rare plants with medicinal attributes,
Taino bracelets and gold crowns
and
Stuffed birds and animals.

Which birds and other creatures they were,
we are not told.
We can only imagine.

The Spaniards marveled at the sights
and uttered oohs and aahs.

The painted Natives didn't say anything.
They were not available for comment.

They may have been simply grateful
that they hadn't been killed and stuffed
by these strange people
who opened their mouths widely when they spoke
and who took more than they needed.

Maybe it was they who needed
to be killed and stuffed.

But it didn't turn out that way
on that particular day.

ZEN

2 Dreams Ago

Signal fires on the horizon.
Undisturbed silence.
Circling the power within oneself.

Need to speak.
But have no mouth to open.
No eyes to see.
No ears to hear.
No tongue to taste.
No hand to touch.

The bridge of return to reality has dissipated.
Nameless ghosts wander across ancient forgotten battlefields.
Nameless ghosts of fallen warriors sit in a circle around a winter fire.
Ancestral territory. Disturbed spirit beings.
Another rhythm of time.
Endless journey.
Luminous curandera remembers what she was doing 25 centuries ago/22
levels of reality.
She taught me the magic.
Equatorial twilight is witness to self-preoccupation/self-transformation.
Shift in perception.
Sudden silence as the sun goes down down down down.
Journey into the underworld.
Profound sense of loss and grief.

Paying homage to Grandmother Moon.
Inside time.
Outside of time.
Under time.
Over time.

And shared genetic memory
is salvaged from the ruins.
And shared genetic memory
is salvaged from forbidden ceremonies.

Salvaged from a land revisited
2 dreams ago.

Reaganomics

I lived in a poor neighborhood.
How poor was it?
They opened up a 99 cent store down the block.
A sign was put in the window.
"We accept layaway."

That's saying something.

Only In New York City

The following exchange took place on the platform
of a New York City subway train station.

"Mommy, look, there's a squirrel on the train tracks"

"Baby child, that is not a squirrel.
Trust me, honey."

Hard Times

Words rooted in blood.
Words rooted in pride.
Words rooted in unkept promises.
Words rooted in channeled spirit power.

Words rooted in shamanic visions.
Words rooted in mysterious dreams.
Words rooted in the tree of life.
Words rooted in the long road to freedom.

Words rooted in surviving prophecies.
Words rooted in the wellspring of the people's reawakening.
Words rooted in patient reconciliation.
Words rooted in nonconfrontational response.

Words rooted in the unspoken power of tribal justice.
Words rooted in the rhythm of reality, timeless reality.
Words rooted in cultural cohesiveness.
Words rooted in the essence of our lives.

The earth speaks, and some of us listen.
The bones of our ancestors call out for assistance.
And some of us understand the need for understanding.
And some of us remember that the dead are often more alive than we.

The twilight deepens.
Look! The future has already ended.
And the past, the past can be seen
In a cage in the market place.

Slave Child

Alone at distant outpost.

Fold your tent.
Fold your aspirations.

She had told you:
"She's your mother.
You're supposed
to tell her the truth.
Three people you
should never lie to:
your doctor
your lawyer
your Mother."

Life is a twisting road
of which war
is a centerpiece,
a prerequisite, some say.

I have learned the meaning of fear
but
am
unable
to comprehend
                    the meaning of silence.

No One

No one call tell our stories
better than we.
Academic posturing.

Making peace with memories/
forgoing bitterness.

Will there ever come a time
when all of us can trace our origins?

First step. You must clear a path within yourself.
In the fullness of time.
With back turned to the future
and the enormity of infinity.

I once met a daughter
who was seeking her destiny.
But she did not know the power
of her given name.

A name she is forever
forbidden
to speak outloud.

An Angel

She is so sweet
that
she smiles in her sleep.

Brain Fever # 2

Limping along on a shoestring budget.
I need a memory. I need a memory right now.
Like an apprentice pickpocket whose business has gone belly-up.
Just glad that the death squad has adjourned to the adjacent room for a card
game.

First teacher saved my bacon,
but she took me to task anyway.
There is always one yo-yo who will rat you out in a second.
That's why nobody knows me by my real name, whatever that is.

The soothsayer has put me on the spot.
Her observations are always on the money,
Sometimes too close for comfort.
She smiles like a fox ready to spring on a fat hen.

Do you remember us?
We are the uprooted trees who seek retribution.
If your name is Juan Ponce de León, hey, I've
got a bone to pick with you.
When White folks first got here,
we marveled when they would curse the wind and the rain.
Didn't they know they were only further antagonizing
these spirits?

Anyone who tells you they're the direct descendent of
Moctezuma is trying to sell you a bill of goods.
A plate of rice and beans with fried chicken on the side, and I'm ready to
go.
But just not yet.
Just not yet.

Solid As A Myth

Ancient stone.
Immortal rock.

Silent teacher
of hu-man.

Vibrating with
unbelievable stories
but having
no tongue to tell.

Death Song

Equatorial twilight.

The great solitude.

Revelation of secrets

reserved for only adept masters.

Inability to focus.

Loss through death.

Fragmentary piece of the future presents herself.

Holding a plume of red smoke in the palm of her hand.

Reconciliation

Why waste time trying to even the score?
We would be remiss in holding on to ancient grudges.
It is a shame that 21st century mythology isn't getting the job done.
I was taught to always know where I was standing and what direction I was facing.

Alternate Realities

There are many levels of realities.
Most of us are only tuned-in on only one or two of them.
That is as much as many of us can handle.

Alternate realities.
Voices of ancient ancestors.
Final instructions imparted through bittersweet tears.

Voices and communiqués from a time before history.
Voices and communiqués demanding a plan of action.

And woman in great pain slowly climbs up a steep hill.

Endurance. Survival. Unacknowledged courage.
Strong memories.
Strong visions.
Dwindling expectations.

Exhume her bones if you dare.

Listen

Eyes of panther.
Mystic smile.

A tree-trunk drum
is heard
from deep in the cedar forest.

Brush with death.
A weary sense of loss.

Time of change
and restlessness.

The land may belong to us.
But the sea – the sea belongs to herself.

Secret Not Worth Keeping

The sun was invited to come down today
after the sky had cleared from a hard rain.

So late in the day.

The smell of the night awaits.
Behind long low hills
and high trees near the river flats.

A last-born child shakes its wings.
It ceases to cry with a broad shrug of the shoulders.
When birds fly we are honored with a gift.

Harvest of fruit.
A tear from the eye.
Take this blessing for a long journey.
A coded message for a maiden voyage.
Send forth this message
that has been spoon-fed by lightning.

Hold your breath.
Listen to the death-camp melody.
It assaults us truly.
so late in a seemingly endless day.

Semantics

Village garden.
Flowers unplundered.

Where is the place
where we now live?
How is it called?

How can you identify a land correctly
when
its original name has been mislaid?

The Quest

In the uncertain light
of a winter solstice celebration
she reveals her identity.

For four moons
she had kept to herself.
A reclusive initiate
at the crossroads of the mind
and the body.

A stark landscape.
Woman astride a stallion
fords a stream in search of
a narrow vision sanctioned
by no one but herself.

Forsaken human prey
abandoned by time and masculine violation.

Remembering
that death has lessons to give us, too.

Remembering
that when time was born
she was given a name
that none can
remember.

Another Yesterday

Pardon me.
I lack a woman's strength.
I lack a woman's patience.

Folks got fed up.
Folks got out of hand.
When they cut off
our line of communications
with the ancestors,
we discovered
we were no longer equal to the task.

Stolen honor.
Hell, man, it was a set-up
        from the get-go.

Time for me to go.
I'm outta here.
I'm scratching all the way around,
and the only answer is
that this poem is a 500 year work in progress.

And I hope to die
in the shade of a ponderosa pine tree.
Just because it sounds like a fine thing
to do.

Raised in the Ancient Manner

Master John
had taught him
the art of sitting.

Master John had told the boy the following words,
"Very often have I sat here in front of my house.
Sitting here for hours without moving.

Sitting here without moving and barely breathing,
I have been able
to see, hear, smell and be in sync with the entire universe.

My master showed me how when I was as child,
and now I show you."

Raised in the ancient manner.
Taught the ancient faith.
Taught out of sight
of those who fear
and do not understand.

Sitting quietly.
Touched by wisdom.
Sitting quietly.
Touched by mystery.

Sitting quietly
Touched by power.

The Wandering Poet Dreamer

The wandering poet dreamer
searches for
alternate cosmic vision
in urban garden
where bloom
flowers of brick and steel.

Ah,
the joy of freedom.
The joy of wandering.

Finding inspiration.
Finding solace.
Finding grandeur in a smile of truth.

Mystic woman.
Compelling thoughts.
Tinkers with magic.
Dreamer in an arid land.

The authorities
keep an eye on her.
She who dares
to share
still-alive poems.
Poetic declarations.

She refuses to be confined.
She refuses to be contained.
She refuses to submit.
She is willing to pay the price.

To Those Who Can Still Believe

By word of mouth.
By sense of smell.
One can tell.
We will come into our own power.

A half-dozen palm-thatched huts
strung along a dirt road
conceal
reveal
a sister town situated in that place
where love and hopelessness converge.

Submissive, yet unconquerable.
Broken, yet unable to be pried loose.
And every setback is a victory.
And every setback is a symbol of resistance.

The spirit of reconciliation
slips through the underbrush
like a leathery iguana.
For audacity cannot be construed as courage
when children pose as divine kings
and assume shadowy identities.

We Shouldn't Be Afraid

We shouldn't be afraid
of songs that speak to the heart.

We shouldn't be afraid
to avoid unnecessary prolonged ordeals.

We shouldn't be afraid
to walk straight forward with our backs straight.

We shouldn't be afraid
to stand tall in the wind.

We shouldn't be afraid
to disremember all the malicious gossip.

We shouldn't be afraid
to sometimes admit that we don't know the score, don't know the agenda.

We shouldn't be afraid
to sometimes walk alone, alone.

We shouldn't be afraid
to not buy into THEIR way of thinking.

We shouldn't be afraid
to occasionally piss off the cosmic forces.

We shouldn't be afraid
to dig into our pockets when approached by a panhandler.

We shouldn't be afraid
to break the news
to break the chain of command
to break the pattern of abuse.

We shouldn't be afraid
to pay attention
to the signal fires
burning on the horizon.

We shouldn't be afraid.

The Other

Respecting the realities of others.
We all have had unique historical, cultural and spiritual experiences.
It can't be expected, therefore, for us to share the same values and/or opinions.
And, remember, nobody escapes unresolved traumas.
Nobody.

Since the beginning there were always differences.
The folks who lived in the cave across the valley or on the other side of the mountain were "the other."
Things were never perfectly in balance.
Understanding contradictions.
Accepting imperfections.

Act in the moment.
Live in the moment.
Laugh in the moment.
Die in the moment.

Not easy to Re-identify.
Not easy to Co-exist.
Separate destinies.
The past has a presence
and it's time to turn it loose

Respecting the realities of others.
This is our dilemma.
Not to confuse disconnection with condescension

Respecting the realities of others.
In the context of who we are,
peace can only be reached when we see ourselves in "the other."

They Told Me

They told me not to read Lorca
because he was a communist.

They told me not to admire the art of Dali
because he was a fascist.

They told me not listen to the music of Leonard Bernstein
because he was gay.

They told me not to study James Baldwin
because he was educated in the Bronx.

They told me not to read Tolstoy
because he was a pacifist.

They told me not enjoy the cinema of Kurosawa
because he loved war.

They told me not to pay attention to Hemingway
because he was a misogynist.

They told me not to pay homage to the poetry of Rumi
because he was a Muslim.

"Stay home," they say, "and watch reality tv.
Only then will you be safe."

South of Yesterday

Night of the kill.
River of death.
Mythical beast
lumbers back to
subterranean lair.
Trailed by a flight of vultures.

Bury him properly.
Carefully wash the bones.
The liberated soul
must not catch fear
on its journey.

It's time
for something sweet.
Feed the departed with smooth rum.
Feed the departed with cakes and
with the blood that speaks
right to your face.

The lords of
the seven spiritual realms
ornament the new arrival
with a crown of bird down and feathers.

Night of the kill.
The assassin
in a loincloth of indigo blues.

Sorrow Conferred

She lives in her heart.

Pain is pain.
And that is why
she has learned
to hide her secrets.

The rocks speak out.
They speak in a voice
that rushes out
from the past.

Lips of stone
whisper thunder song.

RED ROAD

Hip Hop Indians

Hip Hop Indians
rapping in Navajo, Cherokee and Taino.
Spreading the word
with old/new rhythms
that many of their elders
are unable to comprehend.

Hip Hop Indians
rapping in Nahua, Mohawk and Apache.
Utilizing a computerized drum
and thereby disconcerting
the children of Elvis Presley rock and roll jitterbuggers.

Hip Hop Indians,
ain't nothing wrong with your style.
Each generation's got its own unique voice,
                                    Its own unique anger.

Hip Hope Indians,
go on, take care of business.
The spirits will take you where you're supposed to go.

But be careful not to lose the old songs,
the timeless rhythms of your nations.

Flying on the wings of
rap, hip hop, punk rock is cool.
But don't lose the connection to the ancestors.
Remember them?
Remember the stories about the folks who lived way back in them olden days?

Hip Hop Indians
rapping in Taino, Cherokee and Navajo.
You're making your contribution.
You're inventing your own brand new colors.

And it's magic
And it's alive.
And it's yours.   And it's ours.

A Prophet Was Born This Morning

Time to pay homage.
Time to ponder
the true measure of a human being.

A prophet was born this morning
A prophet was born this morning.
She will be a master teacher.

Her destination
will be the path that leads
to balance, even and clear.

Child opens her eyes.
She opens her eyes
sees the cobalt sky.

Her way of life will be
Beauty
harmony
and much much pain.

A prophet was born this morning.
A prophet was born this morning.
Her dreams will be fed with loneliness.

The torch has been passed on.
Thanks to the flesh of many, many mothers.

The people knew before she was born
that she would be special.
The people knew
because she had been heard
crying inside her mother's womb.

Nature in its own time
will transform her into a priestess.

Nature in its own time
will show her that
when freedom is lost

61

one must take courage
and not fear the road to death.

Nature in its own time
will reveal to her
that fire is her brother
and the south wind her steadfast sister.

A dusky child
With tight, curly hair and hazel eyes.
Midwife with hands
brown, dry, hard and leathery.

Midwife sings early morning song
that embraces the day with its truth.

A prophet was born this morning.
A prophet was born this morning.

One day she will sit on a tree stump
and stories will flow out of her
smooth and sweet.

A prophet was born this morning.
And many will need the light of her wisdom.

The world, you know, is coming to an end .... Again.
And many will flock to her for guidance and for healing.

Music of sky.
Song of earth.

A prophet was born this morning.
A prophet was born this morning.
A prophet was born this morning.
                    A prophet was born this morning.

Lenapehoking

The first person who lived in the Bronx
never wore a hat.

The first person who lived in the Bronx
did not speak English, Spanish or Yiddish.

The first person who lived in the Bronx
did not ever curse the wind, rain or snow.

The first person who lived in the Bronx
did not have to read a history book to know where she came from.

Lost In a Dream

Lost in a dream,
a crippled nation
gazes at the distance,
hoping for a harvest of good memories.

Newcomers convene a council of war
as the King dances in the marketplace
while those who cry are those who die.

Is it better to be on the side of right
or
is it better to be on the right side?

Grandmother cries out that she will fight
until
the blood comes out of her eyes.

Dismembered lapses of memory
lodged deep within undeciphered nightmares.
Good memories go fast.
Good times die quickly.

If there's a light on the horizon,
strike at the horizon before its too late.
Listen to that bird telling us good news.

That old bird.
She can sing the old songs and dance the old steps
which most of us never knew even existed.

And a cradle song puts you to sleep.

It's time to go.
Time to go to the ocean.
I will give you a call
and let you know what she has to say.

Grandfather's Recipes

"Tea of grass for kidney stones.
Lion's ear for fever."

The sage of Camuy
had knocked around for many years.
There was a day when he pitched camp on the isle of Vieques
before it was commandeered and transformed into a bombing range.

"Horse stew can be tasty
when you haven't had any grub for a good stretch."

Then there was that short spell
when home was a shanty
in a Haitian backwater clearing.
Kept his savings in a shoebox.

His parents produced eighteen children.
They had no television in those days.

"We haven't been taking care of Mother Earth,
and so she is going to take real good care of us. Just watch."

"I miss the days when my teeth were better.
I shuttled back and forth many a time between Mexico and Texas.
Always one step
ahead of the Border Patrol.
When things got too hot I melted into the jungle."

"I'm usually slow-footed this time of morning.
It takes awhile
for the magic pills to kick in.
Remember,
Virginia Snakeroot for snake bite.
Slippery elm for sore throat."

"One day in the deep, deep past,
Orowama stood on the ocean shore
pondering upon the miseries
being experienced by his people."

History Was Not On Our Side

The three ships came from across the sea.
Raging waters.
Bitter reflections.
They took us for all that we had.

No, history was not on our side
on that inauspicious October day.

And as the sun went down,
tears were heard in the great silence.

****

Cities of the dead.
Tumbled walls.
Ancient stone ruins.
Howling wind. Growing darkness.

Yet, in the graves lie many who refused
to betray the soul of their nation.
Yet, in the graves lie
those whose defeat
was a glorious victory song.

Torn hearts.   Broken promises.

Spirits slowly descending in their journey to the underworld.
Dream spirits demanding to be heard.

And every time that history repeats itself,
the price gets higher and higher.

Brain Fever

A garrison of cultural refugees marches down Pilgrim Road.
Working feverishly to remake themselves in the image of Mister Large-In-Charge.

To hell with the poor!
They deserve everything they don't get.

The guardians of the sacrosanct knowledge are really pissed off.
Devious wizards, the twin brothers have broken ranks.

The day before tomorrow the rent is due.
What happened to the money? I don't know.

The good witch waxes poetically.
She has tantalizing thighs and a beautiful wife.

They want us to leave or disappear.
But we are determined to stay for the duration.

Is tradition big enough to accommodate change?

Can't take a chance/can't take a risk.
The lines of communication have broken down, and ancient hatreds make front page.

Don't be afraid of the day.
The light won't kill you, but your fears might.

Fragmented community limping along. A shoestring operation.

The challenge is to be able to answer the call for action.

Storytelling is a ritualistic privilege.

A burden is a blessing/a souvenir and keepsake.

Some of us have forgotten the melody of the tune which is our birthright.

It's in the Beat

Larry One Hand recalls
his younger days.

"Our drum group had the strongest beat
south of the Canadian border.

When they heard our drum,
It was so strong
that pregnant people
would jump out of bed
to dance."

Atzlán

Atzlán
Tawantinsuyu
Borikén
Tihuanaco.

Vicuña blood ceremonially sprinkled
on fertile dark soil.
Mask maker, with skin of black velvet.
Dream maker, under a deep trance,
appeases spirits unseen.

Cochabamba
Quisqueya
Cuba
Me-xi-ca.

Nighttime stories caution the listener.
Nighttime stories provide guidance.
Just then, red star's reflection startles all.
And moonbeams from the north fills grandfather's breast with pure
euphoria.

Lucayo
Cuzco
Machu Picchu
Michoacán.

Mountain eagle flies off at sunset.
Rain forest hummingbirds/miracle of life/miracle of death.
Voice in the sky.
Breezes of powerful memories blow over the scorched land and deserted
battle fields.

Chichen Itza
Yucatán
Tikal
Uxmal.

Children cry out to the Corn Maiden.

Children cry out to the Plumed Serpent.
Children cry out to the Mother Mesa.   Children cry out.   Cry out.

Oaxaca
Orinoco
Teotihuacan
Bogotá.

Days of joy will return.
Souls of long ago ancestors hard at work.
Falling rain spreads out across hidden valley.
Sea of grass.
Earth colors.
A feast bowl offered to visiting strangers.

And days of joy will finally return to:

Atzlán
Cochabamba
Machu Picchu
and
Uxmal.

A World Apart

"The world is going to end
in fifteen minutes!"

"Are you sure of that?"

"You can bet the house on it."

Fifteen minutes elapse.

"Well, what happened?
We're still here."

"You don't know anything
about Indian time.
Do you?"

La Verdad

You know
that you're hanging out
in a dangerous barrio
when you see
the angel of death
making the sign of the cross
before she turns the corner.

Truth is something
we hear a whole lot about
but very rarely get to hear or see.

A homeless mother
rummages
through a garbage can
and fishes out
a rotten black/red tomato
and
a half-eaten fried chicken leg.

That is truth.
Handle it, baby.

We must prepare ourselves.
The time has come.
I lean into the wind
and follow the steps
of an old Mayan trade route.

A casual observer
takes note
but is unable
to place the scent
as the rocks
begin to speak,
sending a voice
that rushes out from the past.

Steps carry me.
Steps carry me.

Find myself walking alongside
an old woman.
Old woman who lives in her heart.
Old woman who has learned to hide her secrets.
Old woman tired from child bearing.
Old woman tired from grandchildren rearing.

Old woman wears a face of tears,
and one seems to care.

We must prepare ourselves.
The time has come.

Taken Without Permission

The umbilical cord that bound us to the Earth was severed.
Yet, here we still stand.
The land.   Our land.
The land taken without permission.
La tierra sagrada
tomada sin el permiso.

A moment's pause.
False peace.
Teaching moment   passes quietly.

Words out of season.
Flow of time/Lapse of time.
An illusory world.

The land may not be returned.
The broken promises may not be mended.
Yet, First Woman/First Mother, the Maker of All Things,
sits in natural silence.
Waits for our return.

As the young ones are encouraged
to cultivate
a new world
of forgiveness.

Encouraged to return the gift.
Encouraged always to remember,
to
be grateful.

All of My Relations

A mother taught me how to process pain.
A father taught me not to be afraid to disbelieve.
A sister taught me to always be ready to replenish.
A brother taught me to always get the job done, no matter what.

All of my relations.
Field of infinite blessings.

An uncle taught me that the new arrivals did not find a wilderness. They created one.
An aunt taught me why it's important to honor/nurture/value.
A grandmother taught me that many of our finest minds have been remanded to correctional facilities.
A grandfather taught me that those who follow always are behind.

All of my relations.
Act in unity with purpose and resolve.

A son taught me that no one is unworthy.
A daughter taught me never to drown in regret.
A friend taught me to know when to give myself to the waters.
An enemy taught me the importance of recognizing people who walk with the power.

All of my relations.
The eyes of our souls have lost their power to see what is truly right and what is truly wrong.
The eyes of our souls have lost their power to see what is truly right and what is truly wrong.

Beginning Without End

Some of us may die before this evening is over.
A few of us may not die until a half-century from this moment.

We might have the opportunity to break out in spontaneous song.
We might only have the opportunity to shout out, "Oh, shit, no! Not me! Not yet!"

Spirit woman makes the transition confronting the adversary within herself.
Portal signs to the spirit world are not bilingual. ENGLISH ONLY.

Return to sacred place where life constantly begins.

Can dead people read?
Can dead people write?
Can dead people sing a song?

Child of my heart,
we know only one law.

Clean your mind of what you have been told.

Honor the wisdom of the white-haired elders.
Honor the enthusiasm of the young ones.
A life of secrets finally end, for now.

We Talk You Listen

Rediscovering ourselves
five hundred years
after the fact.
We navigate through uncharted waters
In defiance
of the new world order
of old world patriarchs.

We talk
You listen.

In tribute to our fallen ancestors
we deploy warriors to ferret out
the truth of our histories.

Beware. The spirit behind
the massive book burning
of the works of Aztec scribes
still lives today.

We talk.
You listen.

To reconstruct the jigsaw puzzle
of our misplaced legacy,
we summon the ghosts of
our long ago forebears,
pleading that they
provide us with
a brilliant light
to illuminate our re-emergence
from 500 years of darkness.

We talk.
You listen.
Ancient flame of knowledge and wisdom
burns unceasingly.

We talk.
You listen.

We are owed
a five century old debt..

Murder. Rape. Theft. Cultural Confiscation.

The due date
for payment of this bill
is rapidly approaching.

And we are coming to collect.

WE ARE COMING TO COLLECT.

Time to Let Go

Almost out of breath.
Old woman sings
old woman's song.

Walking in a circle,
creating medicine power.
Saving the blood.
Saving the spirit.

Ancestors
speak to her in dreams.

Dreams that flow clearly
in a language that floats away,.

Old woman.
Her true name is known only by herself.
Her death song
is a victory song.

She lies down on a woven straw mat.
Her arms hold on tightly to her wedding blanket.

Time to go.
Time to let go.

Relentless

The spirits of Corn Mountain
sense our approach.
A sanctuary,
a site of secret understanding.

Rocky elevation,
its master
is the Plumed Serpent.

Mother Mesa
of red and white sandstone.
Unforgotten ceremonial
keeps baseless fear at bay.

Mumbled password.
Food offering left on the altar.
A present of yellow beans.
Appropriate tribute.

Access which at one time
had been denied
is now granted.
Recognized vow.
Shouldered responsibility.

Expedition in the night air
Is finalized
near the outskirts
of a central mountain town.

People of the Good.
They walk unimpeded.
They are true to their words.

They may speculate,
but never will they hesitate.

In the Light of Justice

We once all lived at peace with ourselves.
Without fear of living under someone else's protective custody.

We once all lived at peace with ourselves.
Without fear of seeing time as a burden.

We once all lived at peace with ourselves
In close proximity to what made us truly human.

We once all lived at peace with ourselves.
Original identities still intact and whole and decidedly homegrown.

We once all lived at peace with ourselves.
Not using our gender, age or tribal affiliation as an excuse for failure.

We once all lived at peace with ourselves.
Without repudiating/deprecating the natural flow of life.

We once all lived at peace with ourselves.
Sovereign communities with genuine authenticity.

We once all lived at peace with ourselves.
Hands of Sky.
Voices of Earth.
Maintaining the center and
Looking forward to returning to the Light.
Looking forward to returning to the Light.

We once all lived at peace with ourselves.

Gentle Teacher

She speaks in English.
She sings in Spanish.
She dreams in Quechua.
She cries in Yoruba.

Gentle teacher
with songs that speak to the heart.
With songs that speak to the heart.

Very often
I have words for her.
And she listens most carefully
to what I am not saying.
Woman listens to my deep silences.

****

Gentle teacher
activates the love.
And I honor her code
of absolute secrecy.

Looks at me
with eyes of Panther.
Mystic smile.

A Face of Tears.

****

Gentle teacher asks,
"What is death?"
"¿Qué es la muerte?"
All it takes is one quick step
and one short breath.
Time to go.
Time to let go
Dreams that flow clearly.
In languages that float away,

leaving a taste on the tongue.
A taste of cold, pure water.

She speaks in English.
    The 'enemy's tongue'
    Awakens swirling energies.
She sings in Spanish.
    Songs of defiance and
    Victorious defeat.
She dreams in Quechua.
    Sueños de sangre y huesos.
    Dreams of blood and bones.
She cries in Yoruba.
    Tribal ancestry unforgotten.
    Spiritual insight.
    Returns to the light.
    Returns to the light.

She
    speaks in English.
She
    sings in Spanish.
She
    dreams in Quechua.
She
    cries in Yoruba.

With songs
that speak to the heart.

Gentle teacher.

Note: Quechua is a language spoke by many indigenous peoples who originate from the Andes mountains region of South America.

Yoruba is a language spoken by millions of West Africans.

Don't You Wanna Be a Star?

They had come to him
and taken him to their hotel suite.

They talked.
He listened.

"We've been following you," said the first man.
"You're a powerful speaker.
Your voice mesmerizes audiences.
You've got a strong presence, genuine charisma."

"Add it all up," said the second man.
"And we've got a package that we can sell on the market.
It's the right time, and you're the right person
in the right place, backed up by the right people – us."

"For beginners," said the first man.
"We'll get you bookings at all the New Age centers
in major cities from coast to coast.
You'll conduct workshops on Taino spirituality,
raise people's awareness, and all that."

The second man piped up.

"Then we'll hook you up big time.
Audio cassettes.
DVD's. CD's. A book deal.
We'll get you on the conference circuit.
That's a gravy train you've got to jump on.
What do you say?"

The reply from the dark-skinned man came swiftly.

"I am not a whore!
My people's spirituality cannot be packaged to be sold
on the TV home shopping network.

Many of my ancestors were killed
for conducting their sacred ceremonies.
What little knowledge I do have is not for everyone.
It is to be shared only with those who are supposed to receive it."

The two men offered him a cigarette
and asked him to take time to reconsider their offer.

He turned down the cigarette
and marched out in a rush.
He didn't want to miss the last bus to his part of town.

Continuing Saga

I remember
this one Mohawk woman.

She once told me
that her people
used to take
great pride
in their knives
whose blades
were so sharp
that they
could peel off
one layer of your skin
and
you wouldn't shed
one drop of blood.

I
don't know
if
she was pulling my leg
or not.

But
from there on in,
whenever I stayed over
at her place,
I'd sleep
with one eye open
and my feet
right next
to the door.

The Crazy Barber
El Barbero Loco

I wish I had known
Moctezuma's barber.
It would have been
a pleasure to shake his hand.

Moctezuma,
the controversial head honcho of the Aztecs.
He who got railroaded
by Hernán Cortés,
wore a perfectly shaped
goatee beard
without
a hair
out of place.

And even though
Moctezuma did meet
            with a ghastly end.

He left behind many a legacy
            Including a crazy barber's
            masterpiece:
the classic understatement
                    of Moctezuma's goatee beard.

We Honor Who We Were

A crust of bread
A need to dream
A need to live
A need to die
Journey of renewal
Prophesized by our elders
In the early beginnings
Of first light
Revered wolf
Inspirational ally/valued mentor
Awakens nocturnal spirits
With midnight howling
Commitment to remember
Elders – source of power
Eloquent narrative
Endangered language
Sequestered spirituality
Seclusion offers insight
We believe in the land
Not in the corporations
We believe in the purity of the air
That our children breathe
We honor who we were
We honor who we are
We honor who we are going to be
Looking for balance
Who are your people?
Where did your path begin?
Guidepost to a greater reality
Looking for/needing a new reality
Never forgetting to pay
Attention to tomorrow
A crust of bread
A need to dream

Evaluation

Ceremonial thanksgiving.
Baking a loaf of corn bread.
Worshiping in the eye of the sun.
Dropping tobacco offerings on the river bank.
Fasting for four days up on a mountain up Montana way.
Mopping the floor in Cell Section C in the state penitentiary.

All activities equally sacred
and vital
if done
with purpose
with clarity
with simplicity
with honesty.

Quiet the mind in solitary transformation with no illusionary expectations.

War Dance

On an island in the Pacific Ocean,
on the eve
of the invasion
of Okinawa, Japan,
back in the year
nineteen hundred and 45,
warriors
from the nations
Comanche, Pima, Crow, Pueblo,
Kiowa and others,
performed their respective war dances.

Paint
and
cloth of different colors
were provided by the Red Cross.

To create their regalia,
the warriors
used whatever was
at hand:
      rifle cartridges
       coconut and sea shells
       chicken feathers
        ration cans.

These men
were from the First Marine Regiment.
And after the dance
they prophesized
that the casualties
in the upcoming battle
would be not as many
as military intelligence had reckoned.

And the warriors were proven right – naturally.

Tsalagi

"The Ku Klux Klan killed my father
when I was but six years old."

The woman who was honoring me with
her life story was a Cherokee elder.
Her voice was not tinged with sadness.
Having a tragedy filled life
often goes with the territory of being an Indian.

"My husband was Apache.
We were together more than forty years.
Towards the end of his life, he was very sick.
I had to give up working for two years
to stay home and take care of him.
I didn't mind.
And this happened not too long ago.
I'm only just now getting back on my feet."

She laughed and told me that she hoped
that I had good stories to tell her.
And she took her seat in the audience
who had come to hear the storyteller tell tales
from Indian America, North and South.

So I told them stories from the Seneca,
the Maya, the Aztec, and my own Taino.
I told them the story of the Bear Child,
the tale of Viracocha, and the five hundred year old Taino tale
of Matú the Manatee.
And I didn't neglect to share
the Mohawk version of The Origin of Turtle Island.

And when it was over,
everyone walked away except for her.
The Cherokee elder thanked me for taking her back
to the happy days of her childhood
when her grandparents told her some of the same stories.

And her expression of gratitude
made my day.
Her thank you
was a confirmation
of my spirit mission on the this earth.

And you can't ask for much more than that.

The Sand Woman

Had a weird dream last night/early this morning.

I was walking across a deserted beach
when I happened upon a woman sitting on the sand.

She was whittling a piece of wood
into the shape of a snake.
The woman was whittling this stick and was talking to herself.

I sneaked up close to her to try to overhear what she was mumbling.
But I couldn't make out what she was saying.

She suddenly turned her head around and looked dead at me.
Though she was apparently an Indian woman, her eyes were blue.

"Maybe she's an old Mandan," I thought.
"The Mandan were said to have Welsh blood
from long ago travelers to this land."

She started talking to me.
She spoke to me in her own language, but I understood the words.

"I was heard crying In my mother's womb," she said in a proud voice.
"When I was a child the people saw me talking to night birds.
They sent me to live with my grandmother because
they knew that she would raise me better."

The woman stopped talking.
She resumed the task of whittling the stick.
I felt bold. I asked her a direct question.

"So, what's that got to do with me?"

The woman looked at me as if I were stupid.
She handed me the snake stick, rose to her feet and walked away into the ocean
water, disappearing from sight.
I looked at the snake stick which she had given me.

The face of the serpent was my face, eyeglasses and all.

I then heard a voice in my head.
It was the voice of the blue-eyed Indian woman of the sea.

"The weather is going to turn wicked soon," said the voice.
"But it will get right again.
The end of this time cycle is rapidly approaching.
The dwellers of the four corners of the world
are checking you out."

"So, you think you're ready
to be a custodian of the old knowledge?
Well, here is your first lesson,
and it's the important lesson of all.
Remember that you can't listen and talk at the same time."

I dropped the snake stick.
It fell on the burning sand
and it was transformed into a chocolate ice cream bar
that immediately melted away.
All that was left of the chocolate ice cream bar was a stick.

I sat upon the sand,
picked up the stick
while mumbling to myself
and waited
for another fool like myself
to come strolling by.

Hear Our Voices

Long-ago words
Captivating still-alive stories
Gathered insights
Broken memories

Holding our world together by sharing our stories

Does that resonate for you?

Talking about what is truly important.
Talking about what is truly true.
Talking without violating traditional protocol
Talking with reverence
Talking without hard feelings
Talking without forsaking heritage
Talking with loyalty to all creation

Talking
Talking
Talking after only taking time to listen to the silence and drawing power from the stillness of thought.

Tradition

Is tradition big and strong enough to accept change?
That interrogative statement merits attention.

Some are afraid to take chances/take risks.
The dialogue between people and the earth have broken down.
Misguided retaliation by fragmented community.

Famous last words of Christopher Columbus, Al Capone and Richard Nixon:
"I am responsible, but I am not guilty"

We Once Knew

We once knew who we were.

Dynamics of forced assimilation.
Trauma of spiritual genocide.

We once knew who we were.
We once knew
that all we had to do was sit quietly
and listen to the knowledge that lived
in our bones.

We once knew who we were.
This house stood here
long before the first book was ever written.
This house stood here
when the earth was still young and soft.
This house stood here long before.
Man forgot he was born of Woman.

We once knew who we were.
One Nation of many minds and only one heart.

My grandfather grew up in the Indian side of the town of A-ra-si-bo.
Very often he would sit on a wooden bench in front of his hut.
Sitting for hours without moving.

Sitting there completely still he was able to
see, hear, smell and feel the entire universe.
His grandfather had taught him the secrets when he was a boy.
And then he taught me.

We once knew who we were.
Now some of us live in the South Bronx Reservation.
So, watch your step. Watch your ass.

Out of the Silence

Karina tells me
of an apparition that she saw
in the swampland.

A wizened grandmother
in a deerskin dress
and a cornbread necklace.

Snowbird visitation.
Not to be taken lightly.
A gift.
Not a folly.

Extinguished candles.
Journey of awakening.
No need for authority figure.
No need as the landscape sings to your spirit.

APPENDIX

Recommended Books on the Puerto Rican Experience in New York City

1. "A Puerto Rican in New York, and Other Sketches" by Jesús Colón.

2. "Memoir of a Visionary" by Dr. Antonia Pantoja.

3. "Down These Mean Streets" by Piri Thomas.

4. "My Beloved World" by Sonia Sotomayor.

5. "El Bronx remembered: a novella and stories" by Nicholasa Mohr.

6. "When I Was Puerto Rican" by Esmeralda Santiago.

7. "AmeRícan" by Tato Laviera.

8. "Boy Without a Flag: Tales of the South Bronx" by Abraham Rodriguez, Jr.

9. "Memoirs of Bernardo Vega: A Contribution to the History of the Puerto Rico" by Bernardo Andreu Iglesias. Translated by Juan Flores.

10. "Time's Now/Ya Es Tiempo" by Miguel Algarin.

11. "My Life As A Community Activist, Labor Organizer, And Progressive Politician In New York City" by Gilberto Gerena Valentin (Available in English and Spanish)

12. "The Puerto Rican Diaspora Themes In The Survival of A People" by Frank Espada

13. "The Puerto Rican Movement: Voices from the Diaspora (Puerto Rican Studies)" Edited by Andres Torres and Jose R. Velazquez

14. "Aloud, Poetry from the Nuyorican Poets Cafe" Edited by Miguel Algarin and Bob Holman

My Family's South Bronx Bodega

Remember when New York City once teemed with what were called Mom and Pop stores? They are now almost an extinct species. Like the cop walking the beat, the local movie theater, or the neighborhood numbers runner, Mom and Pop business enterprises are on their way out. No one's to blame. Life is about change. And we all have to adjust to the turning of the world.

I am proud to say that my family had one of those Mom and Pop stores. For thirty years, my family owned and operated a bodega on the corner of 154th Street and Courtlandt Avenue, across the street from the Melrose Housing Project. They worked in that bodega for thirty years. Seven days a week. At least fourteen hours a day. In the heart of the South Bronx

How did the phenomenon of the bodega begin? Well, until and during the Second World War, there were Jewish, German and Italian delicatessens all over the city. Sometimes they were passed down from one generation to the next. Often, the children went on to college and became professionals, leaving the family business behind.

After World War II, the demographics in New York City, especially in the Bronx, were transformed dramatically. Almost overnight, a huge wave of migrants from Puerto Rico came here. Important point. Puerto Ricans are migrants. Not immigrants. We are migrants because we are born United States citizens.

Like every other previous group of newcomers, Puerto Ricans had challenges to overcome. My father came here with almost no money, absolutely no knowledge of the English language and a second-grade education. My mother was in almost the same situation, but she at least had a sixth-grade education.

Yes, they had a minimum of formal education. Yet, despite the obstacles, they put all three of us, my two brothers and I, through college. Mami and Papi had almost no schooling. But they had a Ph. D. in love.

In 1948 my father got a job in a restaurant in the West Village in lower Manhattan. The place was called the Twin Brothers Restaurant on the corner of Sixth Avenue and Waverly Place. He labored as a short-order cook and a counter man. After twenty-five years on the job he retired with a pension. Thank God for union contracts!

It was now 1973, and he decided to invest a big chunk of his life savings into a bodega. It was run by Mom and Pop and my two brothers. I was a traveling man so I helped out from time to time through the years.

One of my favorite pastimes in the bodega was sitting down with and listening to the old timers who spun wonderful tales about how it was on Courtlandt Avenue in "the good old days." Courtlandt Avenue, I was told, used to be called Dutch Broadway. Not because any Dutch people lived there. Back in their era, many German immigrants lived on Courtlandt Avenue. The Germans came from "Deutschland," and the non-Germans, therefore, called them Dutch.

My father would tell his own tall tales about Puerto Rico. He claimed that his grandfather Don Segundo never worked a day in his life and was proud of the fact. He made his living from gambling. He and his wife, my great-grandmother, lived a couple of miles outside of a small town called Juncos. Every day, my great-grandfather would stroll to town and look for a card at the local cantina. On one occasion he was caught cheating. The offended party whipped out his machete and cut my great –grandfather across the belly from one end to the other. No problem. He got up, holding his belly together, and walked all the way back home. Upon his arrival, his wife sewed his stomach back together. My great –great grandfather then laid down in his hammock and rested for the three days. On the fourth day he got up and walked the two miles back to town to look for another card game. They don't make them like that anymore.

Mom was the heart of the family. And she was the heart of the bodega. Her job was to keep an eye out for any wise guy trying to sneak a pack of Hostess Twinkies into his pocket without paying. Mom used to say , "Don't look at the smiles on their faces, keep your eyes on their hands."

Mom was everybody's Mami at the bodega. People, both children and grown folks, came to her with their personal problems. A woman with an unfaithful husband. A teenage girl wanting to drop out of high school in order to get a job to help out the family's finances. A man feeling despondent because he had come to this country but had to leave behind his parents, wife, and children. My Mami listened closely to their stories and offered comfort and maternal advice.

I told you that the bodega was located across the street from the Melrose Housing Project. My folks had moved to that project in 1952. So, we got to know at least two or more generations of a number of families in the project.

103

Fast forward to when we got the bodega. One day I observed a young man, who I knew, standing on the corner near the front of the store. He was up to no good standing there. It was obvious that he was, let's say, conducting a shady business. I stepped toward and asked him kindly and softly to take his nefarious undertakings down the block.

He laughed at me and said, "What are you gonna do? Call the cops? I'm not afraid of any police. Ha!"

I got tough. I said, "No, I'm not going to call the cops. I'm going to call you mother. No, I'm telling your grandmother. Better yet, I'm a tell your great-grandmother Miss Betty."

That young man was gone in a cloud of dust. He wasn't afraid of a big, burly cop, but the threat of Miss Betty, his great-grandmother, rolling up her sleeves, ready to whip his behind, put the fear of God into him.

One evening in July of 1977 New York City was hit by a blackout. We were in trouble. No electricity for the refrigerators. All the milk, ice cream and meats and cheeses would be lost. What one of my brothers did was to turn his car around, train the lights on our storefront and provide illumination so we could conduct business.. We stayed open most of the night selling candles, matches, flashlights, batteries and other emergency items.

Meanwhile, the rest of the city was going crazy and some individuals took unfair advantage. The next morning a big panel truck pulled up outside the store. The driver jumped out and asked us if there was anyone interested in purchasing a grand piano. Hmm.

The bodega was in a poor neighborhood. That meant that by the cash register was one of those black and white composition note books where we recorded the accounts due. Many of our clientele lived day-to-day, from hand-to-mouth. Therefore, very often their purchases were 'on the cuff.' We gave credit to those who were struggling, and there were many. I don't know where that composition book is today. There are still many unpaid accounts in that book. But that's okay. Mom and Pop taught us we were put on this earth not to take care of ourselves but to look out for each other.

My mother and father were married for fifty-four years. On my right hand I wear my father's wedding ring. The inevitable happened. My mother suffered a severe heart attack and passed away. Papi lasted one month. He couldn't live without her and left us, too.

One thing I forgot to mention. Toward the end my brothers and I were ready to give up the bodega. The fact is we kept it open mostly to keep my father alive. He had worked non-stop almost every day since the age of ten. And soon after he died, we sold the bodega, closed down the gates, walked away, and we never looked back.

Nevertheless, the memories live on forever in our hearts.

Notes From the South Bronx Reservation

Cherokee. Maya. Apache. Seminole. One by one, they'd walk in, just by chance. Sometimes they knew who we were and needed to visit and chat or simply nod their heads. Their destination was my family's bodega on the corner of 154th Street and Courtlandt Avenue in the South Bronx. We held the fort at that Mom-and -Pop grocery store for thirty years.

Mohawk. Yupik. Taino. Navajo. Indigenous peoples from indigenous nations from North, South, East and West. Our mother was a curandera, a traditional Taino healer with some African thrown in. Counselor and medicine woman who could see your past, present and future. She might lead them to the back room, light up a cigar, and tell them to part company with those who were dragging them down.

Quechua. Narragansett. Montauk. "Black Velvet Indian" from Louisiana. Proud of who they were. No wish to assimilate or change their ways. Some had heard me at a poetry meeting or attended my lecture on 'American History from the Perspective of a Puerto Rican Indian.' One man expressed his gratitude with the gift of a hand-carved walking stick topped with the image of the face of Cotubanamá, ancient Haitian tribal prince. A grandmother bestowed on me a secret name to be shared with no one except the ghosts who appeared in my dreams.

Papago. Kickapoo. Garífuna. Natchez. The store sign read "El Omnipotente." My folks figured that the establishment was a gift of the Great Spirit, so they dedicated the bodega to Him. Some of the local Evangelicals took offense. These weren't Christian Indians seeking our connection. They were traditional Natives steeped in the ways of their most ancient ancestors. Not easily understood by followers of contemporary mainstream faiths. Most of the grocery store's clientele were "Hispanic." However, few were aware of the blood that flowed through their veins. They might have been detribalized and Hispanicized, but they were still Indian.

Choctaw. Lenape. Wampanoag. Miskito from Nicaragua. One young traveler shared a story about his vision quest in the northwest Yellowstone. Taught by an uncle, he spent four days alone in the woods seeking an answer to questions. I explained that my Taino forebears did not practice sweat lodges or vision quests. However, modern day Tainos now were embracing these and other ceremonies of sister Native Nations.

That bodega no longer stands on that corner. My mother and father no longer walk the earth. But I am sure that every once in awhile a Chippewa, Ute, Aymara or Shawnee pilgrim stops and faces the boarded-up, vacant storefront. They will be sure to understand that constant change is an inescapable law of the universe. And they know we will meet elsewhere, at some other point in time in the South Bronx Reservation.

10 Recommended Books on the Indigenous Peoples of Latin America

1. "The Elder Brothers: A lost South American people and their message about the fate of the earth" by Alan Ereira.

2. "Open Veins of Latin America: Five Centuries of the Pillage of a Continent" by Eduardo Galeano.

3. "The Broken Spears: The Aztec Account of the Conquest of Mexico" edited by Miguel Leon-Portilla

4. "Dangerous Memories: Invasion and Resistance Since 1492," a publication of the Chicago Religious Task Force on Central America.

5. "Popol Vuh: the Definitive Edition of the Mayan Book of the Dawn of Life and the Glories of Gods and Kings, with commentary based on the ancient knowledge of the modern Quiché Maya," edited by Dennis Tedlock.

6. "Indigenous Resurgence in the Contemporary Caribbean: Amerindian Survival and Revival," edited by Maximilian C. Forte.

7. "Devastation of the Indies: A Brief Account" by Bartlomé de las Casas.

8. "South American Mythology" by Harold Osborne.

9. "Return of the Maya: Guatemala – A Tale of Survival" by Thomas Hoepker.

10. "Seven Myths of the Spanish Conquest" by Matthew Restall.

www.ingramcontent.com/pod-product-compliance
Lightning Source LLC
LaVergne TN
LVHW021537080426
835509LV00019B/2684